SOUPS & Starters

GW00374391

*For many of us, soups and starters are the best part of any special occasion meal.
The mere sight of a bowl of chilled borscht, its deep red offset by the soured cream
garnish; a beautifully presented salad or seafood appetizer; a golden
glazed grapefruit or a slice of country pâté whets the appetite
and sets the scene for a superb lunch or dinner.
Starters are far too good to be reserved for special occasions, however; light and
easily digestible, they make perfect lunch or supper dishes. Simply adjust
the quantities or reduce the number of servings if more substantial
portions are required. Soufflés, terrines and winter warming soups
can easily double as main course options, especially if crusty bread,
hot toast or a colourful salad is served on the side.
Alternatively, an entire meal can be composed of starters, as is the
practice in many Middle Eastern countries. In Greece and Turkey,
for example, the presentation of these marvellous morsels has almost
been elevated to an art form, with dishes carefully constructed to provide
a palette of contrasting colours and complementary flavours.
Many of the soups and starters in the collection are served cold, to allow
plenty of time for that all-important presentation. Time spent on
setting out a salad or preparing a garnish will be amply repaid
when friends or family survey – and sample – the results.*

CONTENTS

SUMMER SOUPS

When summer sizzles, what better way to start a meal than with a bowl of chilled soup? Whether your choice is for cool green avocado, rich red Gazpacho or the tangy flavour of sour cherries, simple summer soups are certain to prove popular.

Vichysoisse

60g (2oz) butter

2 leeks, sliced

3 spring onions, finely chopped

2 large potatoes, thickly sliced

750ml (1¼pt) chicken stock

155ml (5fl oz) single cream

155ml (5fl oz) natural low fat yogurt

salt

freshly ground black pepper

1 Melt the butter in a saucepan. Add the leeks, with half the spring onions. Cook over moderate heat, without browning, until softened.

2 Add the potatoes and stock. Bring to the boil, lower the heat and simmer for 20 minutes.

3 Purée the vegetables and stock in a blender or food processor until smooth. Transfer the purée to a soup tureen or serving bowl. When cool, stir in the cream and yogurt, with salt and pepper to taste. Chill.

4 Serve in chilled bowls, garnishing each portion with a little of the remaining chopped spring onions.
Serves 6

Variation
Add 90g (3oz) frozen peas with the potatoes. Garnish with mint.

Chilled Avocado Soup

1 large ripe avocado, halved, stoned and peeled

1 tblspn freshly squeezed lime juice

500ml (16fl oz) chicken stock

2 tblspn snipped chives

185ml (6fl oz) single cream

Salsa

½ small onion, quartered

1 drained canned pimiento

1 clove garlic, halved

½ red chilli, seeded

2 fresh coriander sprigs

½ x 410g (13oz) can chopped tomatoes

1 Combine the avocado, lime juice, chicken stock and chives in a blender or food processor. Process until smooth. Add the cream and process for a further 30 seconds, then transfer to a soup tureen or serving bowl. Chill.

2 Meanwhile, make the salsa. Roughly chop the onion, pimiento, garlic, chilli and coriander in a blender or food processor. Add the tomatoes and process briefly until thoroughly combined.

3 Serve the soup in chilled bowls, garnishing each portion with salsa.
Serves 4

Mixed Vegetable Soup (page 9), Chilled Avocado Soup

Chilled Apple and Fennel Soup

Chilled Apple and Fennel Soup

45g (1½oz) butter

2 onions, sliced

1 large fennel bulb, trimmed and sliced, feathery leaves reserved

3 Granny Smith apples, chopped

375ml (12fl oz) chicken stock

1 tblspn snipped chives

155ml (5fl oz) natural low fat yogurt

1 Melt butter in a large saucepan over moderate heat. Add onions, fennel and apples. Cook, stirring constantly, for 3 minutes.

2 Pour in stock. Add chives. Simmer mixture for about 30 minutes, or until vegetables are very soft.

3 Blend or process mixture until smooth. Cool, then stir in yogurt. Chill. Serve garnished with fennel leaves.

Serves 4

Iced Lemon Soup

185ml (6fl oz) lemon juice

pared rind of ½ lemon

1.5 litres (2½pt) chicken stock

3 tblspn cornflour dissolved in 75ml (2½fl oz) cold water

250ml (8fl oz) single cream, chilled

salt

freshly ground black pepper

snipped chives and finely grated lemon rind for garnish

1 Combine lemon juice, rind and chicken stock in a saucepan. Bring to the boil and continue boiling for 5 minutes.

2 Remove lemon rind. Add cornflour mixture, whisking until soup returns to the boil and thickens. Pour into a tureen or bowl. When cool, stir in the cream, with salt and pepper to taste. Chill. Serve garnished with chives and lemon rind.

Serves 4

Cool Carrot Soup

45g (1½oz) butter

1 leek, white part only, sliced

6 carrots, thinly sliced

500ml (16fl oz) water

250ml (8fl oz) freshly squeezed orange juice

1 tspn grated orange rind

salt

white pepper

155ml (5fl oz) natural low fat yogurt

2 tblspn roughly chopped watercress for garnish

1 Melt butter in a saucepan; sauté leek until softened. Add carrots and water. Bring to the boil, lower heat and simmer for 10 minutes or until carrots are very tender. Purée in a blender or food processor, then transfer to a bowl and cool.

2 Stir in orange juice and rind, with salt and pepper to taste. Stir in the yogurt. Chill. Serve with watercress garnish.

Serves 4

Dilled Cucumber Soup

2 cucumbers, peeled, seeded and cut into chunks

1 clove garlic, halved

155ml (5fl oz) natural low fat yogurt

155ml (5fl oz) soured cream

1 tblspn white wine vinegar

3 tblspn chopped fresh dill

salt

freshly ground black pepper

dill sprigs for garnish

Purée cucumbers and garlic with yogurt, soured cream, vinegar and chopped dill until smooth. Add salt and pepper to taste. Chill. Serve garnished portion with a dill sprig.

Serves 4

4

Borscht

This light, clear version of the classic Russian soup is served chilled, with soured cream. For a hot soup, add 250g (8oz) diced steak with the beetroot, and about 125g (4oz) shredded cabbage with the tomato purée. Do not strain the soup, but remember to remove the bay leaf.

500g (1lb) raw beetroot, peeled and roughly grated

1 onion, finely chopped

1.2 litres (2pt) beef stock

1 bay leaf

2 tblspn tomato purée

1 tblspn lemon juice

salt

freshly ground black pepper

about ½ tspn caster sugar

155ml (5fl oz) soured cream or crème fraîche to serve

1 Combine beetroot, onion and stock in a saucepan. Add bay leaf. Bring to the boil, lower heat and simmer for 45 minutes.

2 Stir in tomato purée and lemon juice, with salt, pepper and sugar to taste. Cook for 15 minutes more.

3 Strain soup, pressing vegetables with a wooden spoon to extract as much flavour as possible. Cool, then chill soup until required. Serve chilled, garnished with soured cream or crème fraîche.
Serves 4-6

Kitchen Tips
On chilling, the flavour of Borscht intensifies. Taste the soup just before serving. Add a little more lemon juice, or salt and pepper to sharpen the flavour if necessary. Greek yogurt may be used instead of cream.

Gazpacho

2 tblspn day-old white breadcrumbs

2 cloves garlic, crushed

1 tblspn red wine vinegar

1 tblspn olive oil

1 green pepper, seeded and chopped

1 onion, roughly chopped

5 ripe tomatoes, peeled, seeded and roughly chopped

1 cucumber, peeled and roughly chopped

2 tblspn ground almonds

60ml (2fl oz) tomato purée

1 tblspn chopped fresh parsley

1 Put breadcrumbs and garlic in a small bowl. Add vinegar and olive oil. Mix well, cover bowl and set aside for 2 hours.

2 Combine green pepper, onion, tomatoes, cucumber, almonds, tomato purée and breadcrumb mixture in a blender or food processor. Process briefly, until vegetables are just chopped.

3 Transfer mixture to a large chilled bowl and stir in enough iced water to give soup the consistency of single cream. Cover bowl; chill. Serve topped with chopped parsley.
Serves 4

Traditional Accompaniments
It is customary to offer bowls of croûtons, chopped olives, diced onion, diced cucumber, and finely chopped hard-boiled egg as accompaniments to Gazpacho. Ice cubes are sometimes floated on the soup when serving.

Gazpacho

Chilled Tomato Soup

30g (1oz) butter

2 spring onions, chopped

1 clove garlic, crushed

1 x 410g (13oz) can chopped tomatoes

2 medium avocados, halved, stoned, peeled and chopped

375ml (12fl oz) chicken stock

125ml (4fl oz) natural low fat yogurt

1 tblspn lemon juice

¼ tspn freshly ground black pepper

1 Melt butter in a saucepan over moderate heat. Add spring onions and garlic and cook, stirring, for 1 minute.

2 Stir in tomatoes and avocados. Cook, stirring constantly, for 5 minutes. Stir in stock and simmer for 5 minutes.

3 Purée mixture in a blender or food processor, transfer to a bowl and allow to cool. Stir in yogurt, lemon juice and pepper. Mix thoroughly. Chill. Garnish with fresh herbs.

Serves 4

Chilled Strawberry Soup

375g (12oz) strawberries, hulled

125ml (4fl oz) apple juice

125ml (4fl oz) freshly squeezed orange juice

60ml (2fl oz) natural low fat yogurt

sliced strawberries for garnish

Purée strawberries, fruit juices and yogurt. Pour into chilled bowls, swirl a teaspoon of yogurt on top of each portion and garnish with sliced strawberries.

Serves 6

Fresh Apricot Soup

1kg (2lb) fresh apricots, peeled, stoned and roughly chopped

1 tblspn cornflour

185ml (6fl oz) orange juice

185ml (6fl oz) dry white wine

185ml (6fl oz) natural low fat yogurt

fresh coriander sprigs for garnish

1 Purée apricots. In a cup, mix cornflour to a smooth cream with 60ml (2fl oz) of the orange juice.

2 Put wine, remaining orange juice, puréed apricots and cornflour mixture in a saucepan. Bring to the boil, stirring constantly. Remove from heat; cool.

3 Stir in yogurt. Cover and chill. Serve, garnished with a coriander sprig.

Serves 4

Cold Cherry Soup

750ml (1¼pt) water

250g (8oz) caster sugar

500g (1lb) canned pitted sour cherries, drained

60ml (2fl oz) orange juice

1 tblspn arrowroot

125ml (4fl oz) red wine

125ml (4fl oz) double cream

1 Mix water and sugar in a large saucepan. Bring to the boil, stirring until all sugar dissolves, then boil without stirring for 5 minutes. Add cherries and simmer for 10 minutes.

2 In a cup, blend arrowroot with orange juice. Pour into cherry mixture. Mix well. Simmer, stirring, for 5 minutes more. Cool, then pour into a bowl, cover and chill.

3 Stir in wine just before serving in chilled bowls, decorated with a drizzle of cream.

Serves 4

Chilled Tomato Soup

Garnishes

A sprinkling of chopped fresh parsley is the universal garnish, but there are many more ways of enhancing the appearance of both hot and chilled soups.

Herb sprigs: Mint, chervil and coriander spring to mind, but there are alternatives. Try borage (include flowers and leaves) for chilled cucumber soups, basil or marjoram for any soup that includes tomatoes, a sprig of thyme for a hearty lamb broth. Dill is traditionally used to garnish fish soups; try chopped sorrel for a delicious tangy flavour.

Croûtons: Cubes of bread (white or wholemeal) fried in oil until crisp, croûtons are very popular. The oil may be flavoured with garlic for a robust soup such as Gazpacho.

Fleurons: Puff pastry is used to make these pastry crescents. Roll out the pastry thinly and cut out circles, using a small round cutter or liqueur glass. Move the cutter or glass and cut through each pastry round to create a crescent and a small oval shape from each. Bake the crescents on ungreased baking sheets for about 10 minutes at 200°C (400°F/Gas 6). The oval pastry shapes can either be sprinkled with grated cheese and cooked as savoury biscuits, or re-rolled and cut for more fleurons.

Vegetables: Fine matchsticks, or julienne, of vegetables such as carrots, parsnips and swedes, make an excellent garnish for a clear soup such as consommé. Cook the vegetables briefly in boiling water, refresh them under cold water, then drain thoroughly before floating on the soup. Thinly sliced mushrooms also make a good garnish; there is no need to cook them if serving immediately.

WINTER WARMERS

Comfort in a cup or bowl – that's the simple secret of winter warming soup. Start a meal with hearty Tuscan Bean and Cabbage Soup or creamy Artichoke and Prawn Bisque and there's no need to agonise over afters. A simple salad, filled jacket potato or quiche, followed by fresh fruit, will fit the bill perfectly.

Artichoke and Prawn Bisque

60g (2oz) butter

1 onion, chopped

2 potatoes, cut into 1cm (1/2in) dice

1 x 425g (131/2oz) can artichoke hearts, drained

750ml (11/4pt) milk

1/2 tspn paprika

1/4 tspn freshly ground black pepper

250g (8oz) peeled cooked prawns

snipped chives for garnish

1 Melt the butter in a large saucepan. Add onion and potato and cook gently for 5 minutes.

2 Stir in artichoke hearts, milk, paprika and pepper. Bring soup to the boil, lower heat and simmer for 20 minutes.

3 Purée soup in a blender or food processor, return to clean pan and heat gently.

4 When ready to serve, bring soup to the boil. Set aside a few prawns for garnish and add remainder to the soup. As soon as they have heated through, ladle soup into heated bowls. Garnish with chives and reserved prawns.
Serves 4

French Onion Soup, Artichoke and Prawn Bisque

French Onion Soup

60g (2oz) butter

5 onions, finely chopped

2 beef stock cubes, crumbled

1 litre (13/4pt) water

1 French bread stick, cut into 12 slices

2-3 tspn French mustard

60g (2oz) mature Cheddar cheese, grated

salt

freshly ground black pepper

3 tblspn brandy

1 Melt butter in a large saucepan. Add onions and cook over low heat, stirring occasionally, until golden brown, see Kitchen Tip.

2 Add stock cubes and cook, stirring frequently, for 3 minutes. Stir in water, bring to the boil, then simmer for about 30 minutes.

3 Toast French bread on both sides. Spread one side of each slice thinly with mustard and top with grated cheese. Grill until melted.

4 Taste soup and add salt and pepper as required. Stir in brandy. Serve in heated bowls, placing two or three slices of cheese toast on each portion.
Serves 4

Kitchen Tip
Do not hurry the process of frying the onions. Long, slow cooking ensures maximum flavour.

Mixed Vegetable Soup

Illustrated on page 3

30g (1oz) butter

1 onion, sliced

6 new potatoes, sliced

1.5 litres (21/2pt) chicken stock

2 carrots, cut into matchsticks

2 courgettes, sliced

11/2 small aubergine, diced

90g (3oz) frozen peas, thawed

1/2 red pepper, cut into strips

1/2 green pepper, cut into strips

3 tblspn chopped fresh parsley

1/2 tspn coarsely ground black pepper

1 Melt the butter in a large saucepan over moderate heat. Add the onion and potatoes and cook, stirring frequently, for 5 minutes.

2 Add the stock. Bring to the boil, then lower the heat and simmer for 5 minutes.

3 Add the carrots, courgettes, aubergine, peas, red and green pepper strips, parsley and pepper. Cook for 10-12 minutes, or until the vegetables are just tender. Serve in heated bowls.
Serves 4

Kitchen Tip
Use good quality home-made chicken stock for this soup if possible. Vegetable stock may be used instead, with a 1/2 teaspoon of yeast extract stirred in for extra flavour.

Tuscan Bean Soup

185g (6oz) dried red kidney beans, soaked overnight in water to cover

1 litre (1³/4pt) unsalted vegetable stock or water

125ml (4fl oz) olive oil

2 carrots, chopped

2 sticks celery, sliced

4 courgettes, chopped

1 x 410g (13oz) can chopped tomatoes with basil

3 cloves garlic, crushed

1.2 litres (2pt) chicken stock

250g (8oz) cabbage, chopped

1 Drain beans, put in a saucepan and add vegetable stock or water. Bring to the boil and boil vigorously for 10 minutes. Lower heat and simmer for 1 hour; drain.

2 Heat oil in a saucepan, add carrots, celery and courgettes and fry for 4 minutes. Stir in tomatoes and garlic and cook for 10 minutes, stirring constantly.

3 Add chicken stock and beans. Bring to the boil, then simmer for 30 minutes. Add cabbage and cook for 2 minutes more.
Serves 6-8

Mushroom Soup

125ml (4fl oz) olive oil

6 bacon rashers, finely chopped

125g (4oz) button mushrooms, sliced

1 onion, finely chopped

1.2 litres (2pt) chicken stock

2 potatoes, cut into tiny dice

2 carrots, cut into tiny dice

2 tblspn chopped fresh parsley

½ tspn coarsely ground black pepper

1 Heat the oil in a frying pan. Add bacon, mushrooms and onion. Cook for 5 minutes, stirring occasionally.

2 Bring stock to the boil in a large saucepan. Add potatoes, carrots and bacon mixture. Simmer for 10 minutes or until vegetables are tender. Serve sprinkled with parsley and black pepper.
Serves 6

Parsnip Soup

30g (1oz) butter

2 large onions, chopped

2 tspn caraway seeds

185g (6oz) fennel bulbs, trimmed and chopped

1 large potato, chopped

2 celery sticks, sliced

500g (1lb) parsnips, sliced

1.5 litres (2¹/2pt) vegetable stock

salt

freshly ground black pepper

60g (2oz) mature Cheddar cheese, grated

caraway seeds for garnish

1 Melt butter in a large saucepan, add the onions and caraway seeds and cook over gentle heat for 10 minutes. Add fennel, potato, celery and parsnips. Cook, stirring occasionally, for 5 minutes more until vegetables are lightly coloured but not browned.

2 Add stock. Bring to the boil, lower heat and simmer for 20 minutes.

3 Purée soup in a blender or food processor until smooth. Return to clean saucepan and add salt and pepper to taste. Bring to the boil, then remove from heat and add cheese, stirring until it melts. Serve garnished with caraway seeds.
Serves 6-8

Tuscan Bean Soup, Mushroom Soup

Hasty Chicken Soup

2 litres (3¹/₂pt) chicken stock

1kg (2lb) cooked chicken, finely chopped

1 clove garlic, finely chopped

2 tspn Worcestershire sauce

500ml (16fl oz) single cream

salt

freshly ground black pepper

4 tblspn chopped fresh parsley

4 tblspn snipped chives

1 Bring stock to the boil in a large saucepan. Lower heat and add chicken, garlic and Worcestershire sauce. Simmer for 2-3 minutes or until chicken is heated through.

2 Add cream, with salt and pepper to taste. Stir in herbs. Simmer for 1 minute to reheat, but do not allow soup to approach boiling point. Serve at once, in heated bowls.
Serves 8

Rice and Lemon Soup

1 litre (1³/₄pt) chicken stock

60g (2oz) long-grain rice

60g (2oz) small pasta shapes

1 egg

juice of 1 lemon

1 Bring stock to the boil in a large saucepan. Add rice, lower heat and cook for about 15 minutes or until just tender.

2 Add pasta and cook until tender or *al dente.*

3 Whisk egg in a small bowl. Still whisking, add lemon juice in a steady stream, then add about 250ml (8fl oz) of hot soup.

4 Return lemon mixture to the hot soup, stirring vigorously. Bring to the boil, remove from heat and serve at once, in heated bowls.
Serves 4

Chunky Lamb Soup

Chunky Lamb Soup

30g (1oz) butter

500g (1lb) lamb fillet, cut into 2cm (³/₄in) cubes

1 large onion, chopped

1 tblspn chopped fresh parsley

2 tspn paprika

1 tspn saffron powder

1 tspn coarsely ground black pepper

1.5 litres (2¹/₂pt) lamb or chicken stock

60g (2oz) chickpeas, soaked overnight in water to cover

500g (1lb) tomatoes, peeled, seeded and chopped

4 tblspn lemon juice

60g (2oz) long grain rice

1 Melt the butter in a large saucepan over moderate heat. Add lamb cubes, onion, parsley, paprika, saffron and pepper. Cook for 5 minutes, stirring frequently. Add the stock.

2 Drain chickpeas and add them to pan with tomatoes and lemon juice. Bring to the boil, boil for 10 minutes, then cover pan and simmer mixture for 1-1¹/₄ hours.

3 Stir in rice. Cook for 15-20 minutes or until tender. Serve at once, in heated bowls.
Serves 6

Variation
Use butterbeans instead of chickpeas and substitute 2 sliced leeks for the onion.

Leek Soup

45g (1½oz) butter

3 large potatoes, chopped

6 leeks, thinly sliced

2 onions, thinly sliced

1.5 litres (2½pt) chicken stock

500ml (16fl oz) single cream

1 bunch chives, finely snipped

2 tblspn chopped fresh parsley

salt

freshly ground black pepper

croûtons, optional

1 Melt butter in a heavy-based saucepan, add potatoes, leeks and onions and cook over low heat for 5 minutes.

2 Add chicken stock. Bring to the boil, then lower heat and simmer, covered, until all the vegetables are tender. Cool.

3 Purée soup in a blender or food processor. Return to clean pan, stir in cream and heat through gently. Do not allow soup to boil.

4 Add chives and parsley and stir in salt and pepper to taste. Serve in heated bowls, garnishing each portion with croûtons.
Serves 6

Spinach Soup

30g (1oz) butter

1 onion, chopped

1 clove garlic, crushed

1kg (2lb) spinach, washed, trimmed and roughly chopped

125ml (4fl oz) unsweetened apple juice

125ml (4fl oz) freshly squeezed orange juice

250ml (8fl oz) chicken stock

1 tspn grated fresh root ginger

1 tspn cornflour

125ml (4fl oz) natural low fat yogurt

1 Melt butter in a large saucepan, add the onion and garlic and cook over low heat for 5 minutes.

2 Add spinach, apple juice, orange juice, stock and ginger to the pan. Bring to the boil, lower heat and simmer, covered, for 20 minutes.

3 Purée soup in several batches in a blender or food processor. Return it to clean saucepan. In a cup, mix cornflour and yogurt to a thin cream; pour mixture into pan and mix well.

4 Just before serving, reheat soup gently, stirring constantly. Do not allow it to approach boiling point. Serve in heated bowls, garnished with a drizzle of cream and a dusting of chopped parsley if liked.
Serves 4

Cannellini Bean Soup

220g (7oz) cannellini beans, soaked overnight in water to cover

2 large carrots, sliced

2 onions, sliced

1 stick celery, sliced

1 tblspn tomato purée

1 x 410g (13oz) can chopped tomatoes with basil

4 fresh sage leaves, chopped

155ml (5fl oz) olive oil

3 tblspn chopped fresh parsley

salt

freshly ground black pepper

1 Drain beans, place them in a large saucepan and add cold water to cover. Bring to the boil, boil vigorously for 3 minutes, then drain again. Return beans to pan and once again add fresh water to cover.

2 Add carrots, onions, celery, tomato purée, tomatoes, sage and oil. Bring to the boil, then simmer soup for about 1 hour or until beans are tender.

3 Stir in parsley, with salt and pepper to taste. Cook for 2 minutes more. Serve in heated bowls.
Serves 4-6

Spinach Soup

SOPHISTICATED SALADS

A small, beautifully arranged salad makes a superb starter for a special occasion meal. The emphasis is on colour and flavour in such combinations as Prawn, Avocado and Mango Salad, Ceviche Salad and Italian Salad Platter.

Warm Salad with Italian Sausages

1 Iceberg lettuce

125g (4oz) mixed salad greens (radicchio, lambs' lettuce, sorrel, landcress etc)

2¹/2 tblspn olive oil

8 hot Italian sausages

6 spring onions, sliced

125ml (4fl oz) red wine vinegar

2 tspn Dijon mustard

salt

freshly ground black pepper

1 Arrange the torn salad greens in a large bowl. Set aside.

2 Heat ¹/2 tblspn of the olive oil in a large frying pan. Add the sausages. Fry over moderate heat until golden brown all over and cooked through.

3 Using a slotted spoon, transfer the sausages to paper towels to drain, then cut into 1cm (¹/2in) slices.

4 Reheat the fat in the frying pan; sauté the spring onions for 1 minute. Add the vinegar and bring to the boil, scraping the pan to incorporate any browned bits.

5 Whisk in the remaining oil and add the mustard. Return the sausages to the pan and toss to coat. Add salt and pepper to taste. Pour the contents of the pan over the salad greens, toss well and serve on individual plates.
Serves 4

Radicchio Salad with Sun-dried Tomatoes and Artichokes

1 radicchio lettuce

60g (2oz) fresh parsley sprigs

200g (6¹/2oz) feta cheese, cut into small cubes

¹/2 x 410g (13oz) can artichoke halves, drained and halved

90g (3oz) sun-dried tomatoes in oil, drained and sliced

1 tblspn lemon juice

3 tblspn olive oil

Arrange lettuce leaves and parsley sprigs on individual plates. Top with feta, artichokes and sun-dried tomatoes. Whisk lemon juice and oil together, drizzle over salad and serve.
Serves 4-6

Tomato Basil Salad

375g (12oz) cherry tomatoes, halved

60g (2oz) fresh basil leaves

2 tblspn snipped fresh chives

2 cloves garlic, crushed

1 tblspn lemon juice

3 tblspn olive oil

Arrange tomato halves, basil leaves and chives on individual plates. Whisk garlic, lemon juice and oil together, drizzle over each salad and serve.
Serves 4-6

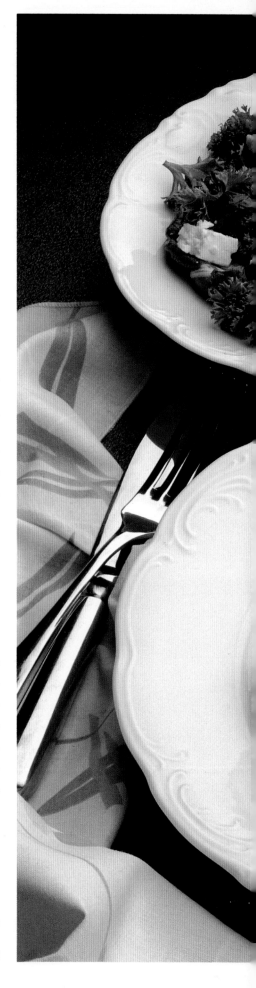

Radicchio Salad with Sun-dried Tomatoes and Artichokes, Prawn, Avocado and Mango Salad

Smoked Chicken Salad

30g (1oz) butter

2 cloves garlic, crushed

4 slices day-old white bread, crusts removed

250g (8oz) watercress sprigs, rinsed and dried

1 smoked chicken, cut into bite-sized pieces

60ml (2fl oz) Vinaigrette Dressing, see Broad Bean and Prosciutto Salad, page 18

1 Melt butter in a small frying pan over moderate heat. Add garlic and cook over low heat for 1 minute.

2 Cut bread into cubes, add to pan and fry until golden. Drain on paper towels.

3 Arrange watercress and chicken pieces on individual plates. Pour over vinaigrette and toss lightly. Arrange a few on top of each salad; serve at once.

Serves 4-6

Prawn, Avocado and Mango Salad

32 cooked prawns, peeled and deveined, tails intact

2 mangoes, flesh cut into thin strips

1 large avocado, flesh cut into thin strips

2 tspn finely grated lime rind

1/2 tspn finely chopped red chilli

1/4 tspn coarsely ground black pepper

2 tblspn lemon juice

3 tblspn olive oil

dill sprigs for garnish

Arrange prawns, mango slices and avocado on individual plates. Combine lime rind, chilli, pepper, lemon juice and oil in a jug. Mix well. Pour a little of dressing over each salad, garnish with dill and serve.

Serves 4

Warm Lettuce and Endive Salad

1 soft round lettuce, torn into bite-sized pieces

1 head curly endive, torn into bite-sized pieces

5 rashers rindless streaky bacon, trimmed and cut into 4cm (1½in) pieces

2 tblspn oil

250g (8oz) button mushrooms, thinly sliced

1 red pepper, thinly sliced

1 small onion, thinly sliced

1 tspn Worcestershire sauce

2 tblspn chopped fresh dill

salt

freshly ground black pepper

60ml (2fl oz) balsamic vinegar

15g (½oz) butter

1 Combine lettuce and endive in a large bowl. Heat bacon gently in a nonstick frying pan until fat runs, then increase heat and fry until crisp. Using a slotted spoon, transfer the bacon to paper towels to drain, then add to salad bowl. Set pan aside.

2 Heat oil in a saucepan. Add mushrooms, red pepper and onion. Stir until heated through. Add the Worcestershire sauce and dill, with salt and pepper to taste. Mix lightly, then add to salad bowl.

3 Return frying pan containing bacon fat to heat. Add vinegar. Bring to the boil, stirring to incorporate any browned bits on bottom of pan. Add butter and stir until melted.

4 Pour dressing over salad, toss lightly and serve at once on individual plates.
Serves 6-8

Smoked Beef and Artichoke Salad

60g (2oz) alfalfa sprouts or cress

8 slices cold smoked beef or roast beef

4 drained canned artichoke halves, halved

¼ red pepper, cut into thin strips

60ml (2fl oz) olive oil

3 tblspn red wine vinegar

¼ tspn coarsely ground black pepper

1 tspn chopped parsley

1 Spread out sprouts on a serving platter. Roll up each slice of beef and arrange decoratively on top. Place an artichoke quarter between each roll and garnish with red pepper strips.

2 Whisk the oil, vinegar, pepper and parsley together in a jug. Drizzle over the salad and serve.
Serves 4

Endive and Avocado Salad

2 avocados, halved, stoned, peeled and sliced

1 head curly endive, torn into bite-sized pieces

125g (4oz) watercress sprigs

60ml (2fl oz) olive oil

3 tblspn lemon juice

1 tspn Dijon mustard

1 tblspn chopped fresh tarragon

1 Arrange avocado slices, endive and watercress sprigs on individual serving plates.

2 Whisk oil, lemon juice, mustard and tarragon together in a jug. Drizzle over each salad and serve.
Serves 6

Smoked Beef and Artichoke Salad

Leek and Quail's Egg Salad

Leek and Quail's Egg Salad

12 quail's eggs, see Kitchen Tip

60ml (2fl oz) olive oil

2 cloves garlic, crushed

2 leeks, white part only, thinly sliced

1 radicchio lettuce, separated into leaves

60ml (2fl oz) Vinaigrette Dressing, see Broad Bean and Prosciutto Salad right

watercress sprigs for garnish

1 Bring a large saucepan of water to the boil. Gently slide in the quail's eggs; simmer for 3 minutes. Drain, cool under cold running water, then refrigerate until required.

2 Heat half the oil in a large frying pan. Add the garlic and leeks and cook over moderate heat for 5 minutes.

3 Arrange the radicchio leaves on four individual plates, with a nest of leeks on top of each. Arrange three shelled eggs on each portion.

4 Whisk the remaining oil and the Vinaigrette together in a small jug. Dress each salad, garnish with watercress and serve.
Serves 4

Kitchen Tip
If quail's eggs are difficult to obtain, use three shelled hard-boiled hens' eggs instead. Cut each egg in quarters.

Broad Bean and Prosciutto Salad

625g (1¼lb) broad beans

185g (6oz) prosciutto, cut into tiny cubes

3 tblspn chopped fresh dill for garnish

Vinaigrette Dressing

2 tblspn red wine vinegar

3 tblspn olive oil

3 tblspn corn oil

1 tspn Dijon mustard

salt

freshly ground black pepper

1 Boil, steam or microwave the broad beans until tender.

2 To make dressing, combine vinegar, oils and mustard in a screwtop jar and shake to combine. Add salt and pepper to taste.

3 Drain beans, place in a bowl and pour over dressing while still warm. Cool, then chill.

4 Just before serving, toss in the prosciutto. Serve garnished with dill.
Serves 6-8

Waldorf Salad with Pecans

2 Granny Smith apples

2 red Delicious apples

2 tblspn lemon juice

6 sticks celery, chopped

60g (2oz) pecan halves, roasted

Dressing

155ml (5fl oz) low fat natural yogurt

1 tspn honey

pinch each of cinnamon and grated nutmeg

1 Core and quarter the apples. Slice them thinly, dip in lemon juice and place in a bowl with the celery and pecans.

2 Whisk the ingredients for the dressing in a jug. Pour over the salad, toss lightly, arrange on individual plates and serve.
Serves 4

Ceviche Salad

24 scallops, rinsed and deveined

90ml (3fl oz) lemon juice

90ml (3fl oz) freshly squeezed lime juice

2 tspn fresh oregano, chopped

1 large red onion, sliced

1 green pepper, chopped

radicchio leaves

1 small cucumber, finely sliced

45ml (1½fl oz) sunflower oil

1 tblspn chopped fresh coriander

1 Rinse and drain the scallops; arrange in a single layer in a shallow dish. Pour over citrus juices and add oregano, onion and green pepper. Toss lightly, cover and refrigerate overnight.

2 Arrange the radicchio leaves on individual plates.

3 Using a slotted spoon, arrange the scallops on the radicchio leaves, tucking the cucumber slices between them.

4 Add the oil and coriander to the marinade, mix well and drizzle over each salad.
Serves 4

Pawpaw filled with Seafood Salad

250g (8oz) salmon

125ml (4fl oz) white wine

125ml (4fl oz) water

250g (8oz) peeled cooked prawns

2 small pawpaws

4 spring onions, chopped

lettuce leaves

1 kiwi fruit, sliced, for garnish

Dressing

125ml (4fl oz) mayonnaise

125ml (4fl oz) single cream

1 tspn tomato purée

dash Tabasco sauce

1 Poach the salmon in a saucepan with the wine and water for about 10 minutes or until cooked. Remove the skin and any bones; flake the flesh and reserve.

2 Make the dressing by mixing all the ingredients thoroughly in a bowl. Add the salmon and prawns, mix lightly, cover and refrigerate for several hours or overnight.

3 Cut the pawpaws in half, remove the seeds and scoop out the flesh, keeping the shells intact. Cube the flesh and add it to the seafood mixture, with the spring onions. Toss lightly.

4 Spoon the mixture into the pawpaw shells, arrange on lettuce leaves on individual plates and garnish with kiwi fruit slices. Serve at once.
Serves 4

Ceviche Salad

Smoked Turkey and Orange Salad

1 head curly endive, separated into leaves
8 slices smoked turkey
1 orange, segmented
1 mango, sliced
125ml (4fl oz) Vinaigrette Dressing, see Broad Bean and Prosciutto Salad, page 18
125ml (4fl oz) freshly squeezed orange juice

1 Make a bed of endive leaves on four individual plates. Arrange the turkey, orange segments and mango slices on top.

2 Whisk the vinaigrette with the orange juice in a jug. Drizzle over each salad and serve.
Serves 4

Tuna, Potato and Watercress Salad

1 bunch watercress
2 potatoes
1 x 200g (6¹/₂oz) can tuna, drained and flaked
¹/₂ green pepper, sliced
4 cherry tomatoes, halved
125ml (4fl oz) Vinaigrette, see Broad Bean and Prosciutto Salad, page 18

1 Rinse watercress, drain and cut into bite-sized pieces. Place in a salad bowl.

2 Boil potatoes in their skins until just tender; drain. When cool enough to handle, skin and slice. Cool completely.

3 Add potatoes, tuna, green pepper and tomatoes to salad bowl. Pour dressing over and toss lightly.
Serves 4

Kitchen Tip
The salad can be prepared in advance and refrigerated until required, but do not add the dressing until just before serving.

Italian Salad Platter

8 radicchio leaves
2 spinach leaves
4 chicory leaves
8 slices bread
8 slices salami
8 slices mozzarella cheese
1 cucumber
¹/₂ x 410g (13oz) can pimientos, drained and cut into strips
60g (2oz) black olives
60g (2oz) sun-dried tomatoes in oil, drained
1 tblspn chopped fresh basil
125g (4oz) stuffed green olives
8 drained canned baby corn cobs
125ml (4fl oz) olive oil
75ml (2¹/₂fl oz) white wine vinegar

1 Arrange radicchio, spinach and chicory leaves on a large platter. Cut out eight rounds of bread, using a scone cutter. Toast bread rounds. Place a slice of salami topped by a slice of mozzarella on each round of toast. Grill until cheese has melted. Arrange toasts on top of leaves on platter.

2 Using a potato peeler, peel cucumber in long lengthwise strips. Twist each strip, then arrange on platter as shown in photograph.

3 Combine pimiento strips, black olives, sun-dried tomatoes and basil in a medium bowl. Mix well; arrange on the platter. Add green olives and corn to platter.

4 Make a dressing by whisking oil and vinegar together. Drizzle over vegetables on platter, avoiding cheese and salami toasts.
Serves 4-6

Variations
Chunks of tuna are a popular addition to the salad platter, as are slices of hard-boiled egg, possibly topped with strips of anchovy. Sliced tomatoes dusted with chopped basil make an attractive border, perhaps surrounding salami cornets or artichoke halves dressed with lemon juice.

Italian Salad Platter

FIRST FRUIT

Make a fresh start with fruit. Light, lovely to look at and not too filling, fruit makes an ideal first course. This chapter includes golden oldies like glazed grapefruit and pawpaw with ginger, plus some tempting new ideas.

Oranges with Avocado

1 curly endive, separated into leaves

2 oranges, segmented

1 avocado, halved, stoned, peeled and cubed

1 spring onion, finely chopped

60ml (2fl oz) freshly squeezed orange juice

1 tblspn lemon juice

3 tblspn oil

2 cloves garlic, crushed

1/4 tspn coarsely chopped black pepper

1 Arrange curly endive leaves, orange segments and avocado cubes on four individual plates. Sprinkle each portion with spring onions.

2 Make the dressing by whisking the orange juice, lemon juice, oil, garlic and pepper in a bowl.

3 Spoon a little of dressing over each salad. Serve immediately.
Serves 4

Kitchen Tip
This salad can be made in advance, if preferred, but should not be dressed until the last minute. Simply sprinkle the avocado cubes with a little lemon juice, cover the plates and refrigerate for up to 4 hours.

Melon Medley

1 mango, cut into cubes

1/2 honeydew melon, cut into cubes

1/2 cantaloupe, cut into cubes

3 tblspn lemon juice

1 tblspn finely chopped fresh coriander

lemon twists for garnish

1 Place mango and melon cubes in a bowl. Pour over lemon juice, sprinkle with coriander and chill for at least 2 hours.

2 Serve in individual bowls or glasses, decorating each portion with a twist of lemon.
Serves 6

Variations
Ogen melons, Charentais or Gallia melons may be used. The important point to remember is that the melons should be ripe and flavoursome.

Pawpaw with Ginger

1 large pawpaw

juice of 1 lemon

45g (1 1/2oz) soft brown sugar

2 tblspn finely chopped preserved ginger

310ml (10fl oz) natural low fat yogurt

1 tspn ground ginger

1 Peel pawpaw, remove seeds and dice flesh. Place it in a large bowl, add lemon juice and toss gently until well coated.

2 Sprinkle sugar over pawpaw and add ginger. Toss lightly. Cover bowl and refrigerate for 2 hours to blend the flavours.

3 Whip yogurt with ground ginger. Spoon pawpaw into individual bowls, top with spiced yogurt and serve at once.
Serves 4

Moroccan Oranges

2 oranges, peeled, pith removed

500g (1lb) carrots, grated

1 tblspn sugar

75ml (2¹/₂fl oz) orange flower water

250ml (8fl oz) freshly squeezed orange juice

60g (2oz) pinenuts, toasted

1 Slice oranges thinly, removing any pips. Place in a bowl with grated carrot.

2 Mix sugar, orange flower water and orange juice in a jug, stirring until sugar has dissolved. Pour mixture over oranges and carrots, cover and set aside for 10 minutes.

3 Toss salad lightly, arrange on six individual plates, sprinkle with pine nuts and serve.
Serves 6

Kitchen Tip
To toast the pine nuts, spread them out on a baking sheet or grill pan and place under a moderately hot grill. Watch the nuts constantly and remove them from the heat as soon as they become golden brown.

Brown Sugar and Rum Glazed Grapefruit

2 yellow or pink grapefruit

60g (2oz) soft dark brown sugar

2 tblspn rum

1 Cut grapefruit neatly in half. Using a flexible serrated knife, carefully cut around each segment, loosening it from skin, but leaving it in place.

2 Sprinkle each grapefruit half with a quarter of the sugar and rum.

3 Place grapefruit under a hot grill for about 3 minutes, or until sugar has melted and is bubbly. Serve at once.
Serves 4

Melon with Prosciutto and Lemon Vinaigrette

Melon with Prosciutto and Lemon Vinaigrette

¹/₂ cantaloupe

20 very thin slices of prosciutto

Lemon Vinaigrette

5 tblspn olive oil

3 tblspn lemon juice

1 tblspn snipped fresh chives

1 tspn coarsely ground black pepper

1 Peel melon, remove seeds and cut flesh into ten 1cm (¹/₂in) thick wedges. Cut each wedge in half crossways; wrap in a slice of prosciutto. When all melon wedges have been prepared, arrange them decoratively on a serving plate.

2 Make lemon vinaigrette by whisking oil, lemon juice, chives and pepper together in a jug. Pour dressing over melon and serve.
Serves 4

Julienne Melon with Lime Mint Dressing

Apricots with Blue Cheese Topping

6 fresh apricots, halved, or 12 drained canned apricot halves

125g (4oz) soft blue cheese

assorted salad leaves to serve

1 Cut fresh apricots in half, carefully removing the seed. If using canned apricots, drain on paper towels.

2 Spread each apricot half generously with blue cheese. Place under a hot grill for about 1 minute or until the cheese melts.

2 Meanwhile arrange a bed of salad leaves on four individual plates. Top each portion with three apricot halves; serve at once.
Serves 4

Variation
Pear halves may be used instead of apricots. Allow two per person.

Icy Mary

2 ripe tomatoes, chopped

2 red peppers, roughly chopped

1 large cucumber, peeled and cut into chunks

6 spring onions, white part only, sliced

1 litre (1³/₄pt) tomato juice

125ml (4fl oz) lemon juice

¼ tspn Tabasco sauce

salt

freshly ground black pepper

6 celery sticks to serve

1 Purée tomatoes, red peppers, cucumber, spring onions, tomato juice, lemon juice and Tabasco in two or three batches in a blender or food processor. Strain into a tall jug and add salt and pepper to taste.

2 Cover jug and refrigerate until well chilled. Serve in tall glasses, with ice if wished. Add a celery stick to each glass to serve as an edible swizzle stick.
Serves 6

Julienne Melon with Lime Mint Dressing

1 small honeydew melon

125g (4oz) large strawberries, cut into small strips

2 tblspn chopped fresh mint

2 tblspn freshly squeezed lime juice

3 tblspn freshly squeezed orange juice

1 tspn honey

1 tblspn sesame seeds

1 Quarter melon, scoop out seeds and remove peel. Cut flesh into 2-3cm (³/₄-1¹/₄in) strips. Arrange melon and strawberry strips in four serving glasses.

2 Combine mint, lime juice, orange juice, honey and sesame seeds in a small bowl. Whisk thoroughly, pour over fruit and serve at once.
Serves 4

Banana and Scallop Kebabs

24 scallops, rinsed and deveined

24 thick slices banana

125g (4oz) butter, melted

1 tblspn chopped fresh coriander

5 tblspn lemon juice

Tabasco sauce, optional

1 Soak six wooden skewers in cold water for 30 minutes. Drain. Thread four scallops and four slices of banana on each skewer.

2 Combine melted butter, coriander, lemon juice, Tabasco to taste in a small bowl. Brush mixture over kebabs.

3 Cook kebabs under a moderately hot grill for 5 minutes or until scallops are just cooked. Turn skewers once and brush frequently with butter mixture.
Serves 6

Spicy Cucumber and Fruit Salad

2 large cucumbers, peeled

½ cantaloupe, seeded

250g (8oz) small strawberries

2 tblspn freshly squeezed lime juice

1 tblspn finely chopped fresh coriander

1 Using a melon baller, scoop the cucumbers and cantaloupe into balls. Place in a bowl.

2 Add the strawberries, lime juice and coriander and mix lightly. Chill before serving.

Serves 4-6

Variations

For a two-melon fruit salad, substitute watermelon balls for the strawberries. Seedless green grapes may be used instead of cucumber, if preferred.

Lemon and Basil Granita

500ml (16fl oz) medium white wine

24 fresh basil leaves, finely chopped

60g (2oz) caster sugar

250ml (8fl oz) lemon juice

1 tblspn grated lemon rind

3 tblspn freshly squeezed lime juice

1 Combine the wine, basil and sugar in a small saucepan over moderate heat. Bring to the boil, then simmer for 3 minutes. Strain the mixture into a jug or bowl and set aside to cool.

2 When the wine mixture is at room temperature, stir in the lemon juice, lemon rind and lime juice.

3 Pour the mixture into ice cube trays and freeze. Remove a few minutes before serving and arrange the cubes in cocktail glasses. Decorate with fresh basil and strawberries if liked.

Serves 4

Lemon and Basil Granita

Spicy Cucumber and Fruit Salad

APPETIZING EGGS AND CHEESE

Some of the easiest – and most economical – starters are based on eggs and cheese. Nothing could be simpler than Eggs Baked en Cocotte or Swiss Cheese Fondue, yet these dishes, together with soufflés, roulades and crêpes, make ideal openers.

Swiss Cheese Fondue

1 clove garlic, crushed

500g (1lb) Gruyère cheese, grated

3 tblspn potato flour

185ml (6fl oz) dry white wine

Dippers

blanched cauliflower florets; blanched broccoli florets; carrot rounds or sticks; celery sticks; button mushrooms

1 Rub around inside of a small fondue pot or flameproof glass saucepan with crushed garlic. Add the cheese, flour and wine. Cook over moderate heat, stirring, until cheese has melted and mixture is thick and creamy.

2 Transfer to a burner or hot tray on the table and serve with dippers speared on fondue forks.
Serves 8

Roquefort Soufflé

60g (2oz) butter, plus extra for greasing

30g (1oz) flour

250ml (8fl oz) milk

100g (3½oz) Roquefort cheese, crumbled

2 egg yolks

7 egg whites

1 Preheat oven to 180°C (350°F/ Gas 4). Melt butter in a medium saucepan over low heat. Stir in flour and cook for 1 minute. Add milk gradually, stirring until mixture boils and thickens.

2 Remove sauce from heat, add cheese and stir until melted. Beat the egg yolks in a small bowl. Add about 90ml (3fl oz) of warm cheese sauce and mix well, then add contents of bowl to saucepan. Beat thoroughly, transfer mixture to a large bowl, cover and cool to room temperature.

3 Grease a 1.8 litre (3pt) soufflé dish with butter. Beat the egg whites in a large grease-free bowl until stiff; fold into the cheese sauce mixture until combined. Pour mixture into greased soufflé dish; bake for 30-35 minutes until well risen and golden brown. Serve immediately.
Serves 4

Variations

Use Cheddar cheese instead of Roquefort if preferred, and add 1 small grated onion to the butter when making the sauce. The mixture may be used to make six individual soufflés; bake these for 20 minutes.

Swiss Cheese Fondue, Roquefort Soufflé

Broccoli and Rice Soufflés

To promote even rising, run a clean thumb around the edge of the soufflé mixture before baking to create a gutter between the mixture and the dish. This stops the mixture from sticking to the sides of the dish as it rises. When making individual soufflés, place the dishes on a baking sheet which has been preheated in the oven. The soufflés will cook more evenly.

Broccoli and Rice Soufflés

60g (2oz) butter, plus extra for greasing
½ onion, finely chopped
30g (1oz) flour
250ml (8fl oz) milk
¼ tspn grated nutmeg
salt
freshly ground black pepper
60g (2oz) Cheddar cheese, grated
125g (4oz) cooked long grain rice
125g (4oz) broccoli florets, blanched and thoroughly drained
3 eggs, separated

1 Preheat oven to 180°C (350°F/ Gas 4). Melt butter in a medium saucepan over low heat. Add the onion and sauté for 2 minutes. Stir in the flour and cook for 1 minute.

2 Add milk gradually, stirring until mixture boils and thickens. Stir in nutmeg and add salt and pepper to taste. Remove sauce from heat, add cheese, rice, broccoli and egg yolks and mix well.

3 Beat egg whites in a large bowl until stiff; fold into broccoli and rice-mixture.

4 Pour mixture into eight greased individual soufflé dishes and bake for 18-20 minutes until well risen and golden brown. Serve immediately.
Serves 8

Asparagus Soufflé

300ml (10fl oz) milk
1 onion, finely chopped
2 blades mace
30g (1oz) butter, plus extra for greasing
15g (½oz) flour
4 eggs, separated
250ml (8fl oz) puréed cooked asparagus
30g (1oz) Parmesan cheese, grated
salt
freshly ground black pepper
2 tblspn fine white breadcrumbs

1 Preheat oven to 180°C (350°F/ Gas 4). Combine milk, onion and mace in a saucepan. Bring to just below boiling point, then remove from heat and stand for 30 minutes. Strain into a jug, discarding contents of strainer.

2 Melt butter in a saucepan, add flour and cook for 1 minute, stirring. Gradually add strained milk, stirring until mixture boils and thickens. Remove pan from heat. Add egg yolks to sauce, one at a time, beating well after each addition. Beat in asparagus purée, then add cheese. Season to taste with salt and pepper.

3 Beat egg whites in a large bowl until stiff. Fold 2-3 tablespoons of egg whites into sauce, then lightly fold in remaining egg whites.

4 Generously butter a 1.5 litre (2½pt) soufflé dish. Sprinkle with breadcrumbs, shaking out excess. Spoon asparagus mixture into dish, taking care not to disturb crumb coating. Bake for 30-35 minutes until well risen and golden brown. Serve immediately.
Serves 4-6

Eggs Baked en Cocotte

15g (1/2oz) butter

4 eggs

salt

freshly ground black pepper

1 tspn snipped chives

1 tspn chopped parsley

4 tblspn single cream

1 Preheat oven to 180°C (350°F/ Gas 4). Using butter, generously grease four individual cocotte dishes. Break an egg carefully into each dish, add salt and pepper to taste and sprinkle chives and parsley on top.

2 Spoon 1 tablespoon of cream over each egg. Bake for 7-10 minutes or until whites are lightly set. Serve at once.
Serves 4

Corn Puffs

30g (1oz) butter

15g (1/2oz) flour

375ml (12fl oz) milk

30g (1oz) Parmesan cheese, grated

125g (4oz) drained canned sweetcorn

3 eggs, separated

1 Preheat oven to 180°C (350°F/ Gas 4).Melt the butter in a saucepan over moderate heat, stir in the flour and cook for 1 minute. Gradually add the milk, stirring until the mixture boils and thickens.

2 Off the heat, stir in the cheese and corn. Allow to cool for 10 minutes, then stir in the egg yolks. Mix well.

3 Grease six individual soufflé dishes. Beat the egg whites in a large grease-free bowl until stiff. Fold into the corn mixture. Spoon into the prepared dishes. Bake for 15-20 minutes until well risen and golden brown. Serve at once.
Serves 6

Individual Ham and Pineapple Frittatas

30g (1oz) butter

1 onion, finely chopped

1 clove garlic, crushed

125g (4oz) cooked ham, chopped

1/4 tspn finely chopped red chilli

1 red pepper, finely chopped

2 spring onions, chopped

4 canned pineapple rings, drained and chopped

1 tblspn finely chopped fresh parsley

3 eggs

185ml (6fl oz) milk

30g (1oz) mature Cheddar cheese, grated

1 Melt the butter in a large frying pan over moderate heat. Add the onion, garlic, ham, chilli, red pepper and spring onions and cook for 3 minutes.

2 Stir in the pineapple pieces and parsley. Allow the mixture to cool to room temperature.

3 Preheat oven to 180°C (350°F/ Gas 4). Grease four 10cm (4in) individual flan dishes. Whisk the eggs, milk and cheese together in a large bowl. Stir in the ham and pineapple mixture.

4 Pour mixture into prepared dishes.Bake for 20-25 minutes until set and golden.
Serves 4

Variation
Use 8 drained canned apricot halves instead of the pineapple rings.

Individual Ham and Pineapple Frittatas

Stuffed Mushrooms

18 large mushrooms

1 tblspn lemon juice

1 bunch coriander

60ml (2fl oz) white wine

1 large onion, chopped

15g (½oz) butter

salt

250g (8oz) spinach

1 tblspn oil

2 cloves garlic, crushed

100g (3½oz) mild Chèvre or other goat's cheese, diced

1 Preheat oven to 180°C (350°F/ Gas 4). Remove stalks from the mushrooms and chop them finely. Wipe mushroom caps with a damp cloth, sprinkle with lemon juice and set stalks and caps aside.

2 Reserve a few coriander sprigs for garnish. Strip leaves from remaining coriander stalks; chop both leaves and stalks finely and set aside, keeping them separate.

3 Heat wine in a heavy-based saucepan. Add onion, chopped coriander stalks, butter and mushroom stalks, with salt to taste. Cook, stirring constantly, until liquid evaporates.

4 Rinse spinach thoroughly. Cook in a saucepan with only water remaining on leaves until wilted. Drain and squeeze dry; chop finely.

5 Heat oil gently in a frying pan and cook garlic for 2-3 minutes. Add the spinach and cook for 4 minutes more. Stir in mushroom mixture. Off heat, add goat's cheese and chopped coriander leaves and mix well.

6 Using a teaspoon, mound mixture on mushroom caps. Arrange them in a shallow baking dish. Bake for 15-20 minutes or until golden. Garnish with reserved coriander sprigs and serve at once.

Serves 6

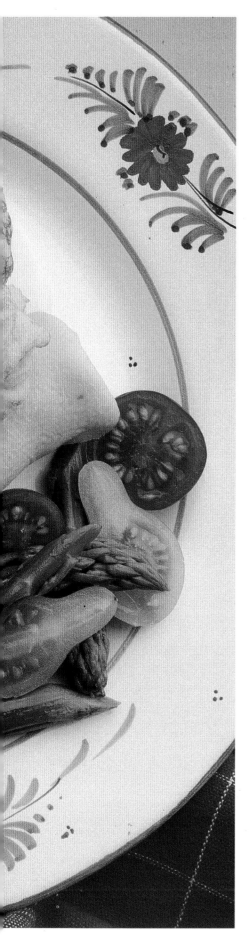

Ricotta and Herb Crêpes

Crêpes

100g (3½oz) butter, melted
440ml (14fl oz) milk
3 large eggs, lightly beaten
125g (4oz) flour

Filling

500g (1lb) ricotta cheese
2 tblspn chopped fresh basil
2 tblspn chopped fresh parsley
30g (1oz) Parmesan cheese, grated
155g (5oz) butter
45g (1½oz) flour
600ml (1pt) milk
60ml (2fl oz) single cream

1 Make crêpes. Melt 45g (1½oz) of butter in a small saucepan. Off heat, beat in milk and eggs. Sift flour into a large mixing bowl, make a well in centre, and slowly pour in egg mixture. Using a wooden spoon, stir mixture, gradually adding flour to make a smooth batter. Cover and set aside for at least 2 hours.

2 Preheat oven to 150°C (300°F/ Gas 2). Melt remaining butter in a small crêpe pan. When butter sizzles, pour a thin layer of batter into pan. Cook for about 1 minute before turning and cooking the other side. Make 11 more crêpes in the same way.

3 Make filling: Put ricotta cheese in a bowl. Using a wooden spoon, beat cheese until softened, then stir in chopped basil and parsley. Add the Parmesan and mix well. Set bowl aside while you make white sauce.

4 Melt 90g (3oz) of butter in a medium saucepan over moderate heat. Stir in flour and cook for 1 minute, then add milk, stirring constantly until mixture boils and thickens. Pour half white sauce into ricotta mixture and mix well.

5 Fill crêpes with herb filling, roll up and place in a shallow ovenproof dish. Reheat in oven. Just before serving reheat remaining white sauce, stir in remaining butter with cream; pour over crêpes.
Serves 6

Tagliatelle with Stilton Sauce

salt
500g (1lb) tagliatelle
125g (4oz) Stilton cheese, crumbled
125ml (4fl oz) soured cream
125ml (4fl oz) mayonnaise
1 clove garlic, crushed

1 Bring a large saucepan of lightly salted water to the boil, add pasta and cook until tender or *al dente.*

2 Meanwhile combine cheese, soured cream, mayonnaise and garlic in a saucepan. Warm gently over low heat, stirring constantly.

3 Drain pasta, place it in a heated serving bowl and pour sauce over top. Toss well to mix and coat. Serve immediately.
Serves 4

Ricotta and Herb Crêpes

FISH FOR COMPLIMENTS

Good looking, quick cooking, fish makes the perfect starter, whether poached, grilled, baked, deep-fried, the star of a splendid salad or served with a creamy sauce.

Taramasalata

60g (2oz) white bread, crusts removed

125ml (4fl oz) milk

2 cloves garlic, crushed

60ml (2fl oz) lemon juice

125g (4oz) smoked cod's roe, skinned

60ml (2fl oz) olive oil

1 Put bread in a shallow bowl, add milk and set aside to soak for 5 minutes.

2 Transfer bread and milk to a food processor. Add garlic, lemon juice and cod's roe. Process until smooth.

3 With motor running, add oil, at first drop by drop, then in a steady stream. Spoon into a bowl, cover and chill for at least 30 minutes before serving with French bread or pitta bread. Garnish with fresh dill if liked.
Serves 4

Avocado with Caviar

2 ripe avocados

3 tblspn lemon juice

200g (6¹/₂oz) cream cheese

3 tblspn mayonnaise

¹/₄ tspn ground nutmeg

2 tblspn caviar for garnish

*Avocado with Caviar,
Taramasalata*

1 Cut avocados in half and remove stones. Using 2 tablespoons of lemon juice, lightly brush avocado flesh to prevent discolouration.

2 Combine cream cheese, mayonnaise and remaining lemon juice in a blender or food processor. Add nutmeg and process until smooth.

3 Divide mixture between avocado halves, filling the cavities. Spoon caviar over top and serve at once.
Serves 4

Prawn Cocktail

shredded lettuce

125ml (4fl oz) mayonnaise

1 tblspn tomato purée

1 tspn creamed horseradish

salt

freshly ground black pepper

250g (8oz) peeled cooked prawns

lemon twists

1 Make a bed of shredded lettuce in four cocktail glasses. Combine the mayonnaise, tomato purée and horseradish in a bowl. Add salt and pepper to taste and mix thoroughly.

2 Set aside four prawns for garnish. Fold rest into mayonnaise mixture. Pile prawn mixture on top of lettuce, garnish with reserved prawns and lemon twists and serve at once.
Serves 4

Scallops with Julienne Vegetables

2 tblspn freshly squeezed lime juice

125ml (4fl oz) dry white wine

2 tblspn coarsely ground black pepper

1/4 tspn sambal oelek or Tabasco sauce to taste

410g (13oz) scallops, rinsed and deveined

2 carrots, cut into thin strips

2 courgettes, cut into thin strips

1 large tomato, chopped

1 tblspn snipped chives

185ml (6fl oz) passata or puréed tomatoes

1 clove garlic, crushed

1 Combine lime juice, wine, pepper and sambal oelek or Tabasco in a frying pan. Bring to simmering point, add scallops and poach for 2 minutes. Remove scallops with a slotted spoon and set aside.

2 Bring a large saucepan of water to the boil, add carrots and courgettes and cook for 1 minute. Drain and refresh under cold water; drain again.

3 Make coulis by puréeing tomato, chives, passata and garlic in a blender or food processor. Strain mixture into a small saucepan and heat gently.

4 To serve, spoon about three tablespoons of tomato coulis onto each serving plate. Decoratively arrange vegetable strips on top and mound scallops in the centre. Serve at once, with a herb garnish if liked.
Serves 4

Deep-fried Crab Balls

250g (8oz) cooked crabmeat, flaked

30g (1oz) butter, softened

2 tspn Dijon mustard

dash of Tabasco sauce

1 egg yolk

3 tblspn fresh white breadcrumbs

salt

flour for coating

oil for deep frying

tartare sauce or fresh tomato sauce to serve

1 Combine crabmeat, butter, mustard, Tabasco, egg yolk and breadcrumbs in a bowl. Mix well, add salt to taste, cover and refrigerate until firm.

2 Shape crabmeat mixture into 18 walnut-sized balls; return to refrigerator for 30 minutes. Roll in flour and deep fry until golden. Drain on paper towels. Serve with tartare sauce on fresh tomato sauce.
Serves 6

Scallops with Julienne Vegetables

Smoked Trout Salad

8 quail's eggs

about 12 mixed lettuce leaves

2 tblspn Vinaigrette Dressing, see Broad Bean and Prosciutto Salad, page 18

125g (4oz) smoked trout, cut into bite-sized pieces

Dill Sauce, see Gravlax, page 37, and brown bread and butter for serving

1 Bring a large saucepan of water to simmering point. Add eggs and simmer for 3 minutes. Drain, cool under cold running water, then refrigerate until required.

2 Toss lettuce leaves with dressing. Divide between four individual plates. Shell quail's eggs and arrange them on salad with trout. Serve with Dill Sauce and bread and butter.

Serves 4

Eggs Stuffed with Tuna

6 hard-boiled eggs, halved

60g (2oz) drained canned tuna

½ Granny Smith apple, finely grated

mayonnaise

curry powder

salt

capers

watercress for garnish

1 Carefully remove egg yolks, keeping whites intact. Mash egg yolks in a bowl.

2 In a separate bowl, mash tuna finely. Stir in grated apple and egg yolks, then add enough mayonnaise to make a creamy paste. Season to taste with curry powder and salt.

3 Spoon or pipe mixture into egg whites; garnish with capers. Serve two stuffed egg halves on each plate, with a watercress garnish.

Serves 6

Octopus Cocktail

Marinated Fish Fillets

500g (1lb) white fish fillets, bones removed and flesh cut into 2.5 x 5cm (1 x 2in) strips

seasoned flour for coating

oil for deep frying

white wine vinegar, see method

3 tblspn chopped fresh parsley

1 tblspn chopped fresh marjoram

1 Dust fish with seasoned flour. Deep fry fish in batches in hot oil for 2 minutes or until golden and cooked. Drain on paper towels; place in a shallow dish.

2 Pour over enough vinegar to cover; stir in the herbs. Cover tightly and refrigerate for 24 hours. Serve at room temperature.

Serves 4-6

Octopus Cocktail

500g (1lb) tenderized baby octopus, heads and beaks removed, cleaned

500ml (16fl oz) water

125ml (4fl oz) lemon juice

2 tspn sambal oelek or Tabasco sauce to taste

125ml (4fl oz) mayonnaise

2 tblspn tomato ketchup

lettuce leaves, sliced avocado and lemon slices to serve

1 Bring water and lemon juice to the boil; add sambal oelek and prepared octopus. Boil octopus for 1 minute or until just cooked. Drain, then chill.

2 Combine mayonnaise and tomato ketchup. Arrange lettuce leaves in four cocktail glasses. Top with octopus, avocado and lemon slices, pour dressing over and serve.

Serves 4

Marinated Prawns Wrapped in Bacon

32 uncooked king prawns, peeled and deveined

60ml (2fl oz) freshly squeezed lime juice

1 clove garlic, crushed

1 tspn grated fresh root ginger

2 tspn soft brown sugar

16 rindless streaky bacon rashers, cut in half lengthwise

1 Soak 16 short wooden skewers in cold water. Place prawns in a medium bowl. Add lime juice, garlic, ginger and sugar and mix well. Cover the bowl and refrigerate for 30 minutes.

2 Wrap one bacon strip around each prawn. Drain skewers and thread two bacon-wrapped prawns on each. Grill for 2 minutes each side or until cooked.
Serves 4

Hot Crabmeat Gratin

500g (1lb) cooked crabmeat

3 rindless rashers thick-cut back bacon, cut in half widthwise

185ml (6fl oz) mayonnaise

1 tspn sweet chilli sauce

1 tspn dry mustard

1/2 tspn Tabasco sauce

1 Preheat oven to 200°C (400°F/ Gas 6). Divide crabmeat between six buttered ovenproof ramekins. Cover with foil and place in oven for 5 minutes.

2 Meanwhile, fry bacon slices in a small frying pan until crisp. Discard foil and place a piece of bacon on top of crabmeat in each ramekin.

3 In a bowl, mix mayonnaise with chilli sauce, mustard and Tabasco. Spoon over crabmeat and bacon mixture. Grill until bubbling. Serve hot.
Serves 6

Prawn Pâté

155g (5oz) butter, softened

500g (1lb) white fish fillets, skin and any remaining bones removed, cut into chunks

500g (1lb) uncooked prawns, peeled and deveined

1/4 tspn grated nutmeg

dash Tabasco sauce

salt

freshly ground black pepper

1 Melt 30g (1oz) of butter in a frying pan. Add fish and prawns. Cook over gentle heat until fish flakes easily and prawns are pink.

2 Place fish and prawns in a blender or food processor with remaining butter, nutmeg and Tabasco. Process until smooth. Season to taste with salt and pepper. Cover and refrigerate. Serve with crackers.

Serves 6-8

Smoked Salmon Moulds

375g (12oz) thinly sliced smoked salmon

125ml (4fl oz) double cream

2 tblspn red lumpfish roe

1/4 tspn cayenne pepper

4 large tomatoes, peeled, seeded and chopped

salt

freshly ground black pepper

2 tblspn snipped chives

1 Line four 7.5cm (3in) moulds with smoked salmon slices. Using clean kitchen scissors, trim away any overhanging bits; purée these with any remaining smoked salmon.

2 Whip cream in a small bowl until stiff. Mix puréed smoked salmon, lumpfish roe and cayenne. Spoon into lined moulds, pressing down well. Cover and refrigerate for at least 2 hours.

Marinated Prawns Wrapped in Bacon

3 Purée tomatoes, with salt and pepper to taste. Loosen salmon moulds by running a thin knife around inside of each. Invert moulds onto individual plates, surround with tomato sauce and garnish with chives.
Serves 4

Gravlax with Dill Sauce

1 side of salmon, scaled and filleted but not skinned

90g (3oz) sea salt

60g (2oz) caster sugar

1/2 tspn freshly ground white pepper

60g (2oz) fresh dill

60ml (2fl oz) brandy

Dill Sauce

125ml (4fl oz) soured cream

125ml (4fl oz) mayonnaise

3 tblspn chopped dill

2 tblspn lemon juice

salt

caster sugar

1 Place salmon on a board, skin side down. Mix salt, sugar and freshly ground white pepper in a bowl, then sprinkle evenly all over fish. Cover with dill.

2 Spread out a sheet of foil large enough to enclose salmon when doubled over. Line foil with cling film. Lay salmon, skin side up, on lined foil, turning edges of foil up to make a lip. Pour brandy around salmon, then bring foil over to make a neat parcel. Place parcel in a dish and place a 1kg (2lb) weight on top. Refrigerate for 3 days.

3 Remove weight and wrappings. Transfer salmon carefully to a board. Scrape off dill and seasoning. Cut salmon diagonally in thin slices, taking it off skin. Arrange on individual plates.

4 To make sauce, whisk together soured cream, mayonnaise, dill and lemon juice. Add salt and sugar to taste. Serve with Gravlax.
Serves 6

Steamed Fish in Radicchio Leaves

Steamed Fish in Radicchio Leaves

500g (1lb) firm white fish fillets, cut into small cubes

1/4 tspn coarsely ground black pepper

1 tspn chopped fresh coriander

1/2 tspn sambal oelek or 1 tspn sweet chilli sauce

2 tblspn freshly squeezed lime juice

16 radiccio leaves

1 Combine fish cubes, pepper, coriander, sambal oelek and lime juice in a bowl. Mix well.

2 Pile one eighth of fish mixture on a radicchio leaf. Cover with a second leaf and make a neat parcel. Tie with cotton.

3 Steam fish parcels over simmering water for 8 minutes or until cooked. Serve two parcels per person, with a herb and lemon garnish, if liked.
Serves 4

Fish Fillets with Lime and Chives

softened butter

750g (1 1/2 lb) cod fillets, cut into six portions

salt

freshly ground black pepper

freshly squeezed juice of 1 lime

12 thin lime slices

60g (2oz) butter, cut into 6 pieces

4 tblspn snipped chives

basil sprigs for garnish

1 Place a large double thickness of foil on the work surface. Spread the foil generously with softened butter.

2 Arrange fish pieces on foil. Add salt and pepper to taste and sprinkle with lime juice. Arrange one lime slice on each fish, topped with a piece of butter. Sprinkle with chives. Reserve remaining lime slices.

3 Bring sides of foil up to make a neat parcel. Cook on a barbecue or under a hot grill for about 10 minutes or until fish flakes easily when tested with tip of a knife.

4 Carefully open foil, retaining juices, and transfer each portion of fish to a heated plate. Remove lime slices, replacing them with fresh ones. Spoon cooking juices over fish, garnish with basil and serve at once.
Serves 6

Deep-fried Sardines

90g (3oz) flour

pinch baking powder

salt

1 egg

75ml (2¹/₂fl oz) water

75ml (2¹/₂fl oz) lemon juice

500g (1lb) whole sardines, fresh or frozen and thawed, cleaned

oil for deep frying

lemon wedges to serve

1 Combine flour, baking powder and salt in a blender or food processor. Add egg, water and lemon juice and process until smooth. Pour batter into a shallow bowl, cover and refrigerate for 1 hour.

2 Coat chilled sardines in cold batter. Deep fry in batches in hot oil until crisp and golden. Drain on paper towels. Serve with lemon wedges.
Serves 4

Sicilian Cod

2 tblspn olive oil

500g (1lb) cod fillet, cut into 3cm (1¹/₄in) strips

1 onion, chopped

4 cloves garlic, crushed

250ml (8fl oz) red wine

2 x 410g (13oz) cans chopped tomatoes with basil

6 large black olives, stoned and thickly sliced

¹/₂ tspn capers

¹/₄ tspn chilli flakes or powder

4 drained canned artichoke hearts, quartered

1 Heat oil in a frying pan. Add fish strips and cook for 1 minute over high heat, shaking pan to sear. Transfer fish to a dish and set aside.

2 Lower heat to moderate, add onion to pan and sauté for 5 minutes. Add garlic and cook for 1 minute more. Add wine to pan and cook until most of the liquid has evaporated. Stir in tomatoes, olives, capers and chilli flakes. Bring to boil, then cook for 5 minutes or until reduced by half.

3 Lower heat to moderate. Stir artichokes into sauce and arrange fish strips on top. Cover pan and simmer until the fish is cooked, about 8 minutes. Remove fish and artichokes to a heated serving dish.

4 Boil sauce until it thickens to a coating consistency. Pour it over fish mixture and serve at once.
Serves 6

Fresh Crab Salad

2 dressed crabs, flesh removed and chopped, claws reserved

2 red chillies, seeded and finely sliced

2 tblspn chopped fresh parsley

3 tblspn freshly squeezed lime juice

60ml (2fl oz) olive oil

¹/₂ tspn freshly ground black pepper

lemon slices for garnish

1 Mix crabmeat with chillies and parsley in a bowl. Whisk together lime juice, olive oil and pepper, pour over crabmeat mixture and toss lightly.

2 Serve on a bed of lettuce, garnished with crab claws and lemon slices.
Serves 6

Fresh Crab Salad

SÂTÉ, PÂTÉ AND TASTY TERRINES

To make the most of meat in the starter stakes, serve small portions on sticks, in slices or as a savoury spread with fresh bread. This chapter has plenty of suggestions, some of them substantial enough to double as supper dishes.

Chicken Saté

You will need about three dozen good quality wooden cocktail sticks for this recipe.

500g (1lb) chicken breast fillets, cut into 2cm (³/₄in) cubes

125ml (4fl oz) water

2 tblspn smooth peanut butter

1 tblspn honey

1 tblspn light soy sauce

2 tblspn lemon juice

1 tspn grated fresh root ginger

1 onion, finely chopped

1 tspn sambal oelek or Tabasco sauce to taste, optional

1 Combine water, peanut butter, honey, soy sauce, lemon juice, ginger and onion in a bowl. Stir in sambal oelek, if using. Mix well. Add chicken cubes, cover and marinate for at least 2 hours or overnight.

2 Soak cocktail sticks in cold water for 30 minutes. Drain. Remove chicken from marinade. Thread two pieces of chicken on each cocktail stick and set aside.

3 Pour marinade into a saucepan, bring to the boil, lower heat and simmer for about 10 minutes, or until sauce is reduced and thickened.

4 Cook chicken for about 10 minutes under a moderate grill or over hot coals, until tender. Serve four satés per person, offering dipping sauce separately.
Serves 8

Lazy Chicken Pâté

500g (1lb) cooked chicken

1 onion, finely chopped

2 hard-boiled eggs, roughly chopped

60g (2oz) ground almonds

2 tblspn brandy

4-5 tblspn mayonnaise

salt

freshly ground black pepper

Tabasco sauce

stoned olives for garnish

1 Chop chicken very finely in a food processor. Add onion, eggs, almonds and brandy and process briefly until well combined.

2 Scrape mixture into a bowl and stir in enough mayonnaise to make a smooth paste. Add salt, pepper and Tabasco to taste.

3 Spoon pâté into a serving bowl or terrine, smooth surface and garnish with olives. Cover and refrigerate until required. Serve with crackers or Melba Toast.
Serves 6

Kitchen Tip
Serve this pâté in tomato shells (scoop out the tomato flesh and use in a soup or sauce) with a salad garnish, if liked.

Chicken Saté

Vitello Tonnato

½ tspn salt

125g (4oz) celery, chopped

1 large carrot, chopped

2 tblspn chopped fresh parsley

½ onion, chopped

750g (1½lb) boned and rolled shoulder of veal, tied with string

185g (6oz) drained canned tuna

250ml (8fl oz) mayonnaise

3 anchovy fillets, drained

2 tblspn capers

60ml (2fl oz) double cream

lemon slices and watercress sprigs for garnish

1 Place about 250ml (8fl oz) water in a large saucepan with the salt, celery, carrot, parsley and onion. Bring to the boil, add the veal and pour in enough water to just cover the meat. Cover the pan and simmer for 1½ hours. Remove the pan from the heat and allow the veal to cool to room temperature in the stock.

2 Make the sauce by processing the tuna with the mayonnaise in a food processor until smooth. Add the anchovy fillets with half the capers; process for 2 minutes more. Transfer the sauce to a bowl and stir in the cream.

3 Slice the veal thinly. Arrange the slices on a serving plate. Spoon the sauce over the top, sprinkle with the remaining capers and garnish with lemon slices and watercress sprigs. Serve.

Serves 6

Vitello Tonnato

Pistachio Nut and Prosciutto Terrine

30g (1oz) fresh white breadcrumbs

2 tblspn dry vermouth

500g (1lb) minced lean pork

500g (1lb) minced veal or turkey

3 tblspn sliced black olives

60g (2oz) pistachio nuts, chopped

60g (2oz) thickly sliced prosciutto, diced

1 tblspn finely chopped fresh basil

½ tspn dried thyme

1 clove garlic, crushed

salt

freshly ground black pepper

1 egg, lightly beaten

250g (8oz) rindless streaky bacon

1 Preheat oven to 180°C (350°F/ Gas 4). Spread out bread-crumbs in a shallow bowl. Add vermouth and soak for 10 minutes.

2 Combine minced meats, olives, nuts, prosciutto, basil, thyme and garlic in a large bowl. Mix well. Season to taste with salt and pepper, add breadcrumb mixture with egg; mix again.

3 Stretch bacon with blunt side of a knife until thin. Line a loaf tin with bacon, allowing some of the pieces to hang over sides. Spoon meat mixture into tin, fold in overhanging pieces of bacon, wrap tin in a double thickness of foil and bake for 90 minutes.

4 Remove tin from oven, discard foil and place a piece of greaseproof paper, cut to fit, on top of terrine. On top of paper place two heavy cans to weight terrine.

5 Cool terrine to room temperature, then refrigerate overnight. Allow to return to room temperature again before carving terrine in slices to serve.

Serves 8

Veal and Spinach Terrine

8 large spinach leaves, washed

45g (1¹/₂oz) butter

2 cloves garlic, crushed

1 onion, finely chopped

4 rindless streaky bacon rashers, chopped

625g (1¹/₄lb) finely minced veal

1 tblspn grated orange rind

2 tblspn chopped spring onions

2 tspn chopped fresh thyme

1¹/₂ tblspn drained green peppercorns

1 tblspn red wine

90g (3oz) day-old white breadcrumbs

2 eggs, beaten

1 x 425g (13¹/₂oz) can apricot halves, drained

1 tblspn lemon juice

1 tblspn apricot jam

1 Put spinach leaves in a large bowl, pour over boiling water to cover and set aside for 1 minute. Drain, refresh under cold water and drain again.

2 Line bottom and sides of a lightly oiled 20cm (8in) cake tin with spinach, reserving enough leaves to cover top.

3 Melt butter in a large saucepan, add garlic and onion and fry for 2-3 minutes. Stir in bacon and cook for 2 minutes more. Stir in minced veal and orange rind; cook for 10 minutes, stirring constantly. Cool mixture slightly, then stir in spring onions, thyme, peppercorns, wine, breadcrumbs and eggs; mix until well combined.

4 Press mixture firmly into prepared tin, cover with reserved spinach leaves and bake for 40 minutes. Cool in tin before cutting.

5 Make apricot sauce by blending or processing apricots with lemon juice and jam until smooth. Press through a sieve. Serve with terrine.

Serves 8

Veal and Spinach Terrine

Pork Rillettes

This rich pâté, made by simmering pork with pork fat until very tender, is a French speciality from the Loire valley.

750g (1¹/₂lb) pork fillet, cut into chunks

1kg (2lb) pork fat, cubed

1¹/₂ tspn salt

freshly ground black pepper

pinch allspice

1 bay leaf

250ml (8fl oz) water

1 Combine all ingredients in a heavy-based saucepan. Bring to the boil, lower heat and cook gently for 4 hours, stirring from time to time.

2 When water has evaporated and meat starts to brown, raise heat and cook until pork fat becomes crisp and golden.

3 Remove meat and pork fat from pan with a slotted spoon, draining off as much fat as possible. Pour remaining fat into a bowl. Discard bay leaf.

4 Place drained meat and fat cubes in a food processor; chop coarsely. Transfer mixture to a bowl and gradually add all but 250ml (8fl oz) of liquid fat. Spoon into small dishes – individual soufflé dishes are ideal – and seal with remaining fat. Cool, then refrigerate until required. Pots or dishes sealed with fat will keep for six weeks in refrigerator.

5 Serve with plenty of crusty bread and a salad garnish. This pâté is very rich; a little goes a long way.

Serves 8

Steak Tartare

You need first class fillet for this dish. Ask the butcher to mince it for you, or chop it very finely in a food processor. It is customary to serve Steak Tartare with a raw egg yolk placed in a hollow in the centre of the meat; if this is the intention, omit the olive oil.

500g (1lb) fillet steak, minced

1 onion, finely chopped

1 tblspn capers, finely chopped

6 anchovy fillets, finely chopped

2 tblspn olive oil

1/4 tspn Tabasco sauce or to taste

salt

freshly ground black pepper

1 Combine the minced steak, onion, capers and anchovies in a bowl. Add Tabasco sauce, salt and pepper to taste and mix well.

2 Divide the mixture into four balls; flatten into patties. Serve with warm toast triangles.
Serves 4

Chicken Liver Brochettes

8 chicken livers, trimmed

24 water chestnuts

12 rashers rindless streaky bacon, cut in half

Marinade

125ml (4fl oz) soy sauce

1 tspn grated fresh root ginger

1/2 tspn curry powder

1 Soak 24 wooden cocktail sticks in cold water for 30 minutes. Drain. Cut each liver into three pieces. Wrap each piece with a water chestnut in a piece of bacon. Thread onto cocktail sticks.

2 Combine soy sauce, ginger and curry powder in a shallow bowl large enough to hold brochettes in a single layer. Add brochettes; marinate for 1 hour at room temperature or overnight in refrigerator.

3 Preheat oven to 200°C (400°F/ Gas 6) for 10-12 minutes, until bacon is crisp and liver is cooked through. Serve four brochettes per person, with a salad garnish if liked.
Serves 6

Cold Lamb Slices with Warm Fig Sauce

2 tblspn oil

1kg (2lb) leg lamb, trimmed

2 spring onions, finely chopped

2 tspn dried thyme

2 tspn flour

185ml (6fl oz) lamb or chicken stock

60ml (2fl oz) red wine vinegar

125g (4oz) fresh figs, quartered

curly endive leaves to serve

1 yellow pepper, cut in strips, for garnish

1 Preheat oven to 180°C (350°F/ Gas 4). Heat oil in a large nonstick frying pan over high heat. Add lamb and brown well on all sides.

2 Transfer lamb to a roasting tin; roast for 1-1¼ hours or until cooked as desired. Transfer lamb to a large dish to cool.

3 Place roasting tin over low heat. Stir in spring onions, thyme and flour, scraping up any bits from bottom of roasting tin. Cook for 1 minute.

4 Gradually stir in stock and vinegar, with half the figs. Bring sauce to the boil, stirring constantly until mixture thickens slightly. Strain into a gravyboat or jug.

5 Arrange curly endive leaves on one large or six individual plates. Slice lamb and arrange slices on endive. Top with remaining figs. Pour warm sauce over top, garnish with yellow pepper slices and serve at once.
Serves 6

Variation
Red peppers, grilled and skinned, make a good addition to this dish.

Beef and Apples with Blue Cheese Dressing

500g (1lb) rump steak

1 tblspn oil

375ml (12fl oz) beer

2 spring onions, chopped

1 green eating apple, sliced

1 red eating apple, sliced

1/2 tspn coarsely ground black pepper

1 tblspn snipped chives

2 tblspn grated horseradish

60ml (2fl oz) mayonnaise

30g (1oz) blue cheese, crumbled

1 tblspn lemon juice

watercress for garnish

1 Brush steak with the oil. Grill in a flameproof dish until medium rare. When cool, slice very thinly, place in a large bowl and set aside.

2 Transfer dish in which steak was cooked to top of stove, pour in beer and heat for 3 minutes, stirring to incorporate any sediment on bottom of dish. Simmer until reduced by one third. Pour mixture into a bowl, cool, then place in freezer for 30 minutes.

3 Add spring onions, apples, pepper and chives to beef slices. Toss well, then arrange on one large or four small serving plates.

4 Remove chilled cooking liquid from freezer. Lift off and discard layer of fat that has congealed on top. Blend or process liquid with horseradish, mayonnaise, blue cheese and lemon juice until smooth. Drizzle over salad, garnish with watercress and serve at once.
Serves 4

Cold Lamb Slices with Warm Fig Sauce, Beef and Apples with Blue Cheese Dressing

Carpaccio with Mustard Mayonnaise

Crostini with Provolone and Salami

1 French bread stick, diagonally cut into 1cm (1/2in) slices

olive oil

2 large cloves garlic, halved

freshly ground black pepper

12 slices salami

12 slices provolone, roughly the same size as the bread

parsley sprigs for garnish

1 Arrange the French bread slices in a grill pan. Place under moderate heat and toast on one side only until golden brown.

2 Remove from the heat, turn the bread slices over and brush the untoasted sides with oil. Rub the cut sides of the garlic over the oiled bread to flavour it, then sprinkle liberally with freshly ground black pepper.

3 Return the bread slices to the grill and toast the oiled sides until golden.

4 Top each bread slice with salami and cheese. Grill until the cheese has melted. Serve hot, garnished with the parsley.
Serves 4

Variations

Try pepper salami with mozzarella cheese or, for a somewhat more humdrum version, ham with Cheddar cheese. Mustard may be spread on the bread rounds before the ham and cheese topping is added.

Carpaccio with Mustard Mayonnaise

500g (1lb) best quality fillet steak, all fat removed, sliced wafer-thin

250g (8oz) assorted lettuce leaves

60g (2oz) watercress sprigs

Mustard Mayonnaise

1 egg

1 tblspn lemon juice

2 cloves garlic, crushed

2 tspn Dijon mustard

60ml (2fl oz) olive oil

60ml (2fl oz) corn oil

1 Arrange beef slices and lettuce leaves decoratively on four individual serving plates. Place the watercress sprigs on top.

2 To make mustard mayonnaise, process egg, lemon juice, garlic and mustard in a blender or food processor until well mixed. Mix oils together. With the motor running, add oils, at first drop by drop, then in a steady stream, until the mayonnaise thickens.

3 Spoon a little of the mustard mayonnaise over each portion of carpaccio. Serve immediately.
Serves 4

Useful Information

Length

Centimetres	Inches	Centimetres	Inches
0.5 (5mm)	$1/4$	18	7
1	$1/2$	20	8
2	$3/4$	23	9
2.5	1	25	10
4	$1^1/2$	30	12
5	2	35	14
6	$2^1/2$	40	16
7.5	3	45	18
10	4	50	20
15	6	NB: 1cm = 10mm	

Metric/Imperial Conversion Chart
Mass (Weight)
(Approximate conversions for cookery purposes)

Metric	Imperial	Metric	Imperial
15g	$1/2$oz	315g	10oz
30g	1oz	350g	11oz
60g	2oz	375g	12oz ($3/4$lb)
90g	3oz	410g	13oz
125g	4oz ($1/4$lb)	440g	14oz
155g	5oz	470g	15oz
185g	6oz	500g (0.5kg)	16oz (1lb)
220g	7oz	750g	24oz ($1^1/2$lb)
250g	8oz ($1/2$lb)	1000g (1kg)	32oz (2lb)
280g	9oz	1500 (1.5kg)	3lb

Metric Spoon Sizes

$1/4$ teaspoon = 1.25ml	
$1/2$ teaspoon = 2.5ml	
1 teaspoon = 5ml	
1 tablespoon =15ml	

Liquids

Metric	Imperial
30ml	1fl oz
60ml	2fl oz
90ml	3fl oz
125ml	4fl oz
155ml	5fl oz ($1/4$pt)
185ml	6fl oz
250ml	8fl oz
500ml	16fl oz
600ml	20fl oz (1pt)
750ml	$1^1/4$pt
1 litre	$1^3/4$pt
1.2 litres	2pt
1.5 litres	$2^1/2$pt
1.8 litres	3pt
2 litres	$3^1/2$pt
2.5 litres	4pt

Index

Editorial Coordination: Merehurst Limited
Cookery Editors: Polly Boyd, Jenni Fleetwood, Katie Swallow
Editorial Assistant: Sheridan Packer
Production Manager: Sheridan Carter
Layout and Finished Art: Stephen Joseph
Cover Photography: David Gill
Cover Design: Maggie Aldred
Cover Home Economist: Annie Nichols
Cover Stylist: Hilary Guy

Published by J.B. Fairfax Press Pty Limited
80-82 McLachlan Avenue
Rushcutters Bay 2011
A.C.N. 003 738 430

Formatted by J.B. Fairfax Press Pty Limited
Printed by Toppan Printing Co, Singapore

JBFP 314 A/UK
Includes Index
ISBN 1 86343 116 0 (set)
ISBN 1 86343 153 5

Distribution and Sales Enquires
Australia: J.B. Fairfax Press Pty Limited
Ph: (02) 361 6366 Fax: (02) 360 6262
United Kingdom: J.B. Fairfax Press Limited
Ph: (0933) 402330 Fax (0933) 402234